CREEPY DOLL MOVIES

Alan Toner

Copyright © 2018 Alan Toner
All rights reserved.

ISBN-13: 978-1729668795
ISBN-10: 1729668798

Other Books By Alan Toner

Hammer Horror Trivia
Hammer Horror Remembered
100 True Ghost Stories
100 True Ghost Stories Vol. 2
Haunted Objects
True Ghost Stories
True Ghost Stories 2
True Ghost Stories 3
True Ghost Stories 4
UK UFOs
Werewolf Nightmare
Horror Stories
Horror Stories 2
Famous Psychics

Contents

1. Why We Love Creepy Doll Movies..................1
2. The First Creepy Doll Movies........................5
3. The Child's Play Franchise...........................10
4. The Puppet Master Movies..........................16
5. Robert The Doll...26
6. Magic 31
7. Anna..33
8. Asylum – Mannikins of Horror 35
9. The Creepy Doll...37
10. Dead Silence...39
11. Dolly Dearest..41
12. Dolls..43
13. Trilogy of Terror.......................................45
14. Annabelle...48
15. Twilight Zone's Talky Tina........................54
Author's Note...56

1. Why We Love Creepy Doll Movies

Why are so many of us horror fans fascinated by creepy doll movies? Why do we spend pounds going to see on the pictures, or buy on DVD or Blu Ray, such movies as Child's Play, Annabelle and The Puppetmaster?

Well, maybe it all goes back to our childhood. When we were very young, dolls represented things that were almost human. Whether it was a grinning clown or a pretty Looby Loo-type, these dolls were our first real playmates, to the extent that we even looked upon them as our faithful companions, just as we would a school friend. A child's imagination, having not yet established a firm grip on reality, is so vast, and absolutely brimming with all kinds of magical ideas and fairytale images. Thus, it is perfectly understandable that if a kid should happen to have a doll in their toy cupboard, then all that wild imagination should run riot in their relationship with that object. You will often hear a child say something like, "Ooo, Mummy, my doll Bunty told me a real funny joke today." It's as if, in that kid's mind, the doll is an actual living person, and not just a wooden toy put together in some toymaker's factory. Of course, not wishing to disabuse their child's dreamy notion that the doll is a real human being, the parent will often just laugh along with the kid and say something like, "Oh really? And what was the joke then?"

On the other side of the coin, there can be a certain doll in the toy collection that can appear rather less lovable to a child than the aforementioned ones. Whether it is the doll's physical appearance (perhaps it's a kind of witchlike doll, with a black cloak and an ugly old face) or just the rather unsettling feeling it generates as a whole, this kind of doll is liable to inspire nightmares in a young child. And we all know just how many weird dolls have been churned out by toy manufacturers over the years, don't we? Halloween immediately comes to mind as the ideal time for a mass-market explosion of creepy looking dolls.

Just as a youngster can imagine lovely things coming from their relationship with their pretty, lovable dolls, so they can quite easily imagine rather less pleasant things coming from their ugly, scary dolls. In the child's dreams (or nightmares), these devil dolls suddenly come to life, jumping off the toy shelf and chasing them all around the bedroom, often brandishing terrifying weapons, Chucky style. Such terrifying scenarios can often ensue in the child suddenly waking up in the dead of night, screaming with fear and shouting for their parents to come rushing into the room to save them from the evil doll that is coming for them.

Let's face it, dolls are, generally, top of the list of child's playthings. Little girls are especially noted for loving dolls, and pretend play with them, which can help in fostering imagination and creativity. But on the other hand, it becomes a matter of great concern and worry for parents when their little daughter suddenly starts crying and screaming at the mere sight of a doll. While most childhood cases of Pediophobia (fear of dolls) disappear once the child has grown, in some cases this fear can persist even into

Creepy Doll Movies

adulthood.

Horror movie makers must certainly bear all this in mind when they are making a creepy doll movie. Childhood fears make for some fantastic scary stories, and what could be more scary than a doll suddenly coming to life and terrorising you out of our mind? And if a doll-on-the-rampage movie, providing the story is good, stands a good chance of making millions of dollars at the box office, then all the more reason to really get into the craft of producing an outstandingly good creepy doll movie that will scare the pants off your audience.

Another factor that certainly comes into the creepy doll genre is the one known as the "uncanny valley" concept. This idea suggests that humanoid objects - including, of course, dolls -, which appear almost like real human beings, elicit uncanny, or strangely familiar, feelings of eeriness and revulsion in observers. You see this motif all the time in creepy doll movies. It's what makes the story work so much. The very idea that that seemingly cheeky grin spread across the ventriloquist's dummy, for example, may also have a certain dark character behind it is the real stuff of nightmares. Great examples of this are found in the eerie ventriloquist doll movies Magic (1978) and Dead of Night (1945), both of which will be covered in more detail later on in this book.

The uncanny valley concept was first hypothesised in 1970 by the Japanese robotocist Masahiro Mori, who identified that as robots take on more human-like attributes, people would find them more acceptable and appealing than their mechanical counterparts. But this idea stretched to only a limited extent, for when robots were close to, but not quite, human, people began to feel less comfortable and more uneasy. Moreover, some even began to feel a little fearful of these human-like robots. If the robot or doll looks a little too human, then it starts to creep people out. It is this distinctive deterioration in the relationship between human likeness and emotional reaction that the term "uncanny valley" arises from. Again, some great fodder here for making a gripping, entertaining creepy doll movie.

Another interesting aspect about a doll is that it seems to have a dead aspect about it. It is just an almost human-like body, but completely devoid of any human life inside. This "dead" aspect can give a doll a real creepy quality, for its eyes are open and forever staring, its expression often frozen into a smile, and it is lifelike. This aspect is often reminiscent of a child's corpse.

Children are much loved and revered in today's society, as they represent pure innocence. But if that inherent innocence is somehow contaminated by something malevolent and evil – especially if that dark force should happen to emanate from a rather creepy-looking doll – then all hell breaks loose, and the innocence of childhood suddenly becomes dangerously at risk. It's the old enhanced contrast theory, which we have seen so much of in horror movies involving youngsters over the years: seemingly innocent but actually quite harmful. Movies involving demonically possessed kids, like The Exorcist, are other examples of this concept.

Anyway, they are just a few suggestions as to why so many of us are fascinated by the creepy doll movie. Let us now move on to discuss the whole history of creepy dolls in the cinema.

2. The First Creepy Doll Movies

The very first creepy doll movie was The Great Gabbo (1929). This was an American Pre-Code early sound production, a musical drama directed by James Cruze and based on a story (The Rival Dummy). The movie starred Erich Von Stroheim and Betty Compson.

The film tells the story of the consummate ventriloquist "The Great Gabbo" (Stroheim), who increasingly uses his dummy "Otto" as his only means of expressing himself. This is a classic example of an artist driven to insanity by his work. Gabbo's unique gimmick is that he is able to make Otto talk and sing while Gabbo eats, drinks and smokes. In the time-honoured tradition of a typical creepy doll movie, Otto has the creepy ability to speak and think on his own – the "almost human" trait I touched on in the first chapter of this book. However, unlike in most creepy doll movies, Otto is not actually evil himself; it's his owner, Gabbo, who is the monster, an insane egomaniac who can't forge a steady relationship or even say a good word about anybody unless he speaks through his dummy. He is the quintessential egotistic actor. And the more Gabbo relies on his dummy to do his dirty work, the more insane he becomes.

Otto's voice was provided by an off-screen actor, and sounds like a lilting singsong little boy, which can be quite irritating at times. Physically, Otto is always smartly attired in suit and tails.

Otto's owner, Gabbo, is a very unattractive man: short, balding, Teutonic. However, his forceful, demanding personality makes up for these physical failings. His voice is loud and sergeant-major authoritative. He even wears a monocle. He does not suffer fools gladly, demanding the very best from everybody. It's not surprising, therefore, that his dummy Otto is his only real friend, and even he can't stand him at times!

When it opened, The Great Gabbo did not exactly generate favourable reviews. Although Stroheim himself did receive good words, the movie did absolutely nothing to boost his acting career.

Because the original copyright holder failed to renew the film's copyright, the movie fell into the public domain, enabling anybody to copy and distribute a VHS/DVD copy. This resulted in many extremely poor-quality copies of the movie being made available on the market. Although colour sequences were shot, only black-and-white versions of the movie remain. The film was originally made as a silent one, but was later transformed to sound as technology advanced in the late 1920s.

The Great Gabbo was very much a movie of its time, replete with 1920s flapper girls, the noticeably incipient stages of movie sound, and musical vaudeville sequences. If you want to know where the very first creepy doll movie sprang from, then this movie is your best starting place.

Moving forward a few years later to 1936, The Devil Doll starred a cross-dressing Lionel Barrymore as an escaped convict who uses miniaturized humans to exact revenge on those who framed him. Directed by Tod Browning and co-starring Maureen O'Sullivan and Frank Lawton, the movie was adapted from the novel Burn Witch Burn (1932) by Abraham Merritt.

Promoted as a novelty thriller, the movie was not a great financial success, although it did get some praise from critics. For example, The New York Times gave it a very positive review, comparing its marvellous special effects to those featured in movies like King Kong and The Invisible Man.

In short, The Devil Doll , though obviously dated, is a thoroughly entertaining tale about bitter revenge and shrunken people.

In 1945, a British horror movie, produced by Ealing Studios, was released which was the first real horror anthology film of the kind later popularised by such studios as Amicus. In addition to offering some really eerie tales with an excellent framing story, this movie had a particularly creepy doll. That doll was called Hugo, and it was featured in the very last story in the anthology, The Ventriloquist's Dummy. Hugo was a ventriloquist doll, and his owner was a rather emotionally unbalanced stage performer called Maxwell Ferere (played superbly by Michael Redgrave, father of Vanessa and Lynn). One night, an American ventriloquist, Sylvester Kee, watches the act, and after the show, Sylvester, invited by Hugo, goes backstage. While Maxwell is away, Hugo suggests that he and Sylvester go into partnership. Although Sylvester seems to warm to the idea, he thinks this is just part of Maxwell's act. However, Maxwell is worried that Sylvester might accept Hugo's proposition. Deeming Maxwell to be insane, Sylvester leaves.

Later on, Sylvester sees Maxwell become involved in a drunken brawl in a hotel bar. Afterwards, Sylvester helps Maxwell to his room, leaving the dummy propped up on the bed. Later on, Maxwell bursts into Sylvester's room, demanding to know where Hugo has been hidden. Sylvester denies any underhanded wrongdoing, and is dumbfounded when Hugo is found. Maxwell shoots Sylvester twice. Maxwell is then arrested and thrown into a cell.

During Maxwell's imprisonment, a psychiatrist, Dr. Van Straaten visits him in his cell and intends to reunite him with his dummy. Hugo seemingly starts to taunt Maxwell about his misfortune, aggravating the ventriloquist so much that he smothers the dummy and stamps it into pieces. As a result of his actions, Maxwell is then locked up in an asylum. Sylvester, having now recovered from his injuries, visits Maxwell. However, the voice that greets him is not Maxwell's, but Hugo's. And the closing scene to this story, where Hugo seems to . . . well, actually come ALIVE, is one of the most memorable and creepy endings I have ever seen.

The ventriloquist's dummy Hugo is, without doubt, a very eerie and disturbing creation. He is the very epitome of the "evil doll", and has been the template for many other horror ventriloquist movies over the years, especially Magic (1978), which starred Anthony Hopkins as a ventriloquist whose disposition was equally as dodgy as that of the Michael Redgrave character in Dead of Night. I have seen quite a few creepy ventriloquist doll movies over the years, but I have to say that the Hugo dummy in Dead of Night is definitely No. 1 on my list of all time scary ventriloquist dolls.

In 1964, another British creepy doll movie was made, only this time, unlike the story in Dead of Night, the whole of the movie centred exclusively on the ventriloquist story. Not to be confused with the 1936 Tod Browning classic "The Devil Doll", whose story is totally different, the film was called Devil Doll, and it starred Bryan Haliday as stage hypnotist and magician "The Great Vorelli". The dummy he employed in his act was (again, just like in Dead of Night) called Hugo. Vorelli regularly performs his act on the London stage. When he meets a gorgeous heiress, he starts to pursue her and, eventually, mesmerises her, sending her into a strange coma. His shapely mistress (Magda) fears he'll dump her for the younger woman, and threatens to expose him. Vorelli tricks Hugo into killing Magda while he's safely elsewhere. When Marianne's boyfriend, Mark, investigates, he uncovers details of another killing in Vorelli's past: that of a man named Hugo. The girl emerges from her coma, and announces her intention to marry the hypnotist. When the victorious Vorelli tells Hugo his plans for Marianne and a new, female dummy, a final confrontation leads to totally unexpected results.

Whilst Devil Doll has no real scenes of violence, the movie is still quite unsettling due to the creepy doll Hugo. Also, the special effects in the movie were very good for their time.

Frederick E. Smith wrote the original story of Devil Doll for London Mystery Magazine in 1951, earning £10 for it. The script was originally written in 1957.

3. The Child's Play Franchise

When horror fans talk about their favourite creepy doll movies, the series of movies that most frequently come to their minds are the Child's Play films. Not surprising really, considering that Child's Play is one of the most popular - if not THE most popular - creepy doll flicks ever made. Chucky, the main character of this franchise, has become, just like Freddy Krueger and Jason Voorhees, something of a cultural horror icon in himself, and the Child's Play movies have spawned countless fan paraphernalia - including, of course, many Chucky dolls.

A major part of Chuck's popularity is no doubt the excellent voice work of Oscar-nominated actor Brad Dourif, who has voiced the evil toy throughout the series

The first Child's Play movie was made in 1988. Directed by Tom Holland, the movie centres on a voodoo practitioner and serial killer called Charles Lee "Chucky" Ray. Whilst being chased by police, Ray is shot by one of the detectives, and as he lies dying, he recalls what he was taught by his voodoo instructor, and uses his amulet, The Heart of Damballa, to transfer his soul into a child-sized Good Guy doll. A homeless peddler subsequently finds the doll and sells it to Karen Barclay, who passes it on to her son, Andy, as birthday gift. But Andy soon discovers that this is not just an ordinary doll, for when Chucky kills his babysitter, he tries to warn people of the doll's malevolent powers. But his efforts prove to no avail, for he is put in a mental institution, and the onus then falls on his mother to try and convince the detective of the doll's murderous powers before Andy becomes Chucky's next victim.

For its time, Child's Play was an outstandingly original movie, with its storyline of a kid's doll being possessed by the soul of a serial killer. The movie attracted much critical acclaim, and did so well at the box office that a sequel, Child's Play 2, was made in 1990.

In Child's Play 2, which is set two years after the first film, the plot centres on serial killer Charles Lee Ray (Chucky) continuing his pursuit of Andy Barclay, who was placed in a foster home, and transferring his soul into him after being resurrected. Jenny Agutter and Gerrit Graham play Andy's foster parents. The movie was released on 9th November 1990, and made an estimated $28.5 million in America. Although it didn't do quite as well as the first Child's Play movie, a third film was made, Child's Play 3, in 1991.

Child's Play 3, occurring eight years after Chucky's death in the previous movie, centres on Andy Barclay's exploits in a military school. But unfortunately for Andy, the demonic doll Chucky has decided to tag along too! The Play Pals Toy Company has decided to re-release its Good Guys line of dolls, believing that as so much time has now passed since the horrific events of the previous movie, all the bad publicity has finally died down. But because they make the mistake of recycling old materials for their new doll range, the baleful spirit of Charles Lee Ray is once more resurrected to wreak havoc embodied in the Chucky doll. As Andy is the only person who is aware of Chucky's evil intentions, he is the only one who can put a stop to the evil doll's menace.

Alan Toner

Chucky returned for a fourth outing in Bride of Chucky (1998). Many fans regard this movie as the start of Chucky's sorry decline as a credible and entertaining horror character, for the movie's plot was so ridiculous and dull that the film has even been deemed the worst Chucky outing ever. Bride of Chucky introduces Jennifer Tilly, who went on to be a familiar and recurring figure in the Chucky franchise, as Ray's long time girlfriend, Tiffany, who stumbles upon a Dummies book on voodoo rituals. She uses the book to summon hellish spirits with a view to reviving Chucky. But unfortunately for Tiffany, things don't go quite the way she planned, and she finds herself trapped in the body of another plastic doll too. Inevitably, the two murderers fall in love again, and proceed to pursue their goal of retrieving the "Heart of Omzilla", an amulet that has the power to enable them to return to their human forms.

Although Bride of Chucky is noted for its brutal slayings, dark, macabre humour, and love-hate relationship between Tiffany and Ray, it still falls well below the standard of all the previous movies in the franchise. But despite that failing, it is still a "guilty pleasure" with a lot of fans.

If Bride of Chucky proved to be a big drop in the fright factor of the killer doll, then Seed of Chucky (2004), plummeted the series to even lower depths. Again, this movie had a lame storyline, and diluted even further Chucky's horror element, just as the later Elm St movies toned down Freddy Krueger's scare element in favour of a more facetious approach. Seed of Chucky, the fifth instalment of the Child's Play saga, is a direct sequel to Bride of Chucky. The story again centres on the murderous exploits of Tiffany and Chucky, both of whom are resurrected by their inoffensive son, Glen. They take a trip

Creepy Doll Movies

to Hollywood, where a film depicting the malevolent dolls' murder spree is being made. Needless to say, all proper family decency is chucked (no pun intended here) completely out of the window as the wicked couple embark on a fresh rampage of murder and mayhem. Glen, horrified by their brutal killings, incurs the disapproval of both Chucky and Tiffany, neither of whom can understand why their son is not following in their malevolent footsteps. Starstruck Tiffany cannot get her head around the fact that the movie will star her favourite actress, Jennifer Tilly, who soon becomes an unwitting host to this new family in more ways than one.

Seed of Chucky features Brad Dourif returning as the voice of Chucky, while Tilly plays both herself and Tiffany. The son of the murderous pair, Glen, is voiced by Lord of the Rings star Billy Boyd. Cult film director John Waters also makes an appearance, as does hip-hop artist Redman. For all its failings, Seed of Chucky is funny, scary in parts, and a wonderful satire of Hollywood and the cult of celebrity.

The real return to form in regard to making Chucky scary again was Curse of Chucky (2013). Departing from the silly, pathetic, humorous overtones that ruined the last couple of movies in the series, Curse of Chucky certainly pulls no punches in delivering what true horror fans really want: plenty of thrills and chills and scares. And the big, creepy house in which most of the story takes place, coupled with the ominous thunder and lightning outside, certainly enhances the generally dark atmosphere of the movie.

The story takes place some time after the events of Seed of Chucky. Nica (brilliantly played by Brad Dourif's daughter, Fiona), a young woman, who has been confined to a wheelchair right from birth, summons her sister, Barb, and her brother-in-law, Ian, for a funeral following the death of her mother. Whilst in the throes of organising this family get-together, Nica receives a strange package. When she opens it up, she finds that it contains a rather creepy-looking doll. Then, when people start getting killed, one after the other, Nica soon comes to realise, to her horror, that her unsolicited mailing is much more than just an ordinary doll. Chucky, voiced again by the incomparable Brad Dourif, is back with a vengeance!

For me, this is undoubtedly the best sequel to the first Child's Play since Child's Play 2. I can watch Curse of Chucky again and again, unlike all the other mediocre sequels. There is plenty of tension, atmosphere and bloodshed, and some great plot twists thrown in for good measure. Also, all the characters are interesting and well portrayed, and you really feel for Nica as she battles the murderous, demonic Chucky in that huge, shadowy house. So, with the original Chucky magic revitalised in Curse of Chucky, I certainly had high hopes for the next movie in the series, namely Cult of Chucky. But, as it turned out, was I disappointed, and here's why.

Cult of Chucky (2017) was a huge disappointment. I hated the way they tampered with the storyline, taking it into new areas which, to be quite frank, should never have even be contemplated. What an utterly stupid idea to start creating clones of Chucky. I ask you! After the brilliance that was Curse of Chucky, I had such high hopes for this movie. Unfortunately, my hopes were soon shattered once I started watching this piece of garbage, and unlike its fantastic preceding movie, this is one that I shall definitely not be watching again.

Creepy Doll Movies

The storyline follows on from the events of Curse of Chucky, with the murderous doll again pursuing wheelchair-bound Nica, who is now locked up in an insane asylum, after having been wrongly accused of murdering her family. At the same time, Chucky has a couple of scores to settle with his old enemies, aided by his former wife, Tiffany. When the dead bodies start piling up, Nica soon realises that her killer doll might not be just some horrific illusion plaguing her mind, but a real menace. And that's not all, for she also discovers that the doll is gradually starting to possess anyone or anything with a view to joining a huge cult to kill off Chucky's victims. Then Chucky's long lost friend, Andy Barclay, turns up at the asylum, and he tries to stop the cult from expanding. However, he also has to contend with the obstacle that is Chucky's deviant wife, Tiffany.

The main problem with Cult of Chucky is that it lacked any kind of good, gripping plot development. The storyline was very weak and far-fetched and, at times, downright annoying. Why the hell do we need more Chucky's when we have already got one? I have never been a big fan of clone stories (look at the way they ruined Spider-Man in the comics by introducing clones of such people as Gwen Stacy), and this is one clone story that certainly ranks in my all time Top 10 of lousy clone tales. After this disappointing, boring, disjointed mess of a movie, I can only hope that the next Chucky film will return to the solid, serious form of Curse of Chucky.

I'm certainly not holding my breath, though.

4. The Puppet Master Movies

Perhaps the most popular creepy doll franchise, after the Chucky one, is the Puppet Master series. And, just like the Chucky films, there have been quite a few Puppet Master movies made since the first one was released back in the late 1980s. The Puppet Master films, as have the Chucky movies, have also earned themselves something of a cult status with fans of creepy doll flicks.

    The first movie in the franchise, Puppet Master, was made in 1989 by Full Moon Productions, a company created by Charles Band. Although the movie was initially intended for theatrical release, it was ultimately put out as a straight-to-video production in October 1989, as Band opined he would stand to make more money this way than he would in the cinema market. The story opens with a scene involving an old but consummate puppet maker called Andre Toulon (William Hickey), who is forced to commit suicide by shooting himself in the mouth as he is hounded by the Nazis in World War Two whilst in the throes of putting the finishing touches to a new puppet called Jester at the Bodega Bay Inn. Toulon had been no ordinary puppet master, for he had discovered a powerful means to make puppets come to life using ancient Egyptian techniques and a mysterious potion. This was a secret he carried with him to the grave. But there was a dark side to Toulon's work, for when the puppets came to life, they instantly became

Creepy Doll Movies

predatory, murderous little creatures, each with their own deadly unique abilities, like vomiting leeches or drilling holes in people's bodies.

Flash forward 50 years later, and the story now focuses on a group of psychics, who make contact with an old colleague of theirs, Neil Gallagher, and believe that he has found Andre Toulon's hiding place. When the psychics investigate the Bodega Bay Inn, scene of Toulon's suicide, they find that Toulon's puppets, once thought long lost, are still at large, and have abandoned none of their hellish desires to indiscriminately maim and kill any unfortunate who happens to cross their path.

Whilst Puppet Master isn't a great film, it is still a good-old-fashioned-puppets-on-the-rampage yarn, full of fun and sure to delight any fan of creepy doll movies. It has excellent special effects in terms of the stop-motion puppets coming to life and embarking on their murderous activities, and has some superb set pieces, all enhanced by generous dollops of blood and gore here and there. The human characters are also interesting and quirky, and balance off well against the group of puppets they interact with, each of which has its own unique abilities - and, boy, do these nasty little buggers put these abilities to some lethal use too! Of all the puppets, I found the Leech Woman to be the most unlikeable and repulsive, whilst my favourite puppet was the little stripe-jerseyed man with the drill on his head. I also liked the Andre Toulon back-story, which brilliantly provided the origin of the animated puppets. Loved the ending too.

In 1990, a sequel was made to Puppet Master, entitled Puppet Master 2. Again, just like the first film in the franchise, this was released directly to video. Puppet Master 2 sees the return of the malevolent little dolls we first got acquainted with in Puppet Master. This time, they stalk and terrorise a group of US paranormal researchers for their brain fluid, which they plan to pass on to their master, Andre Toulon. He needs the brain serum to resurrect his wife. Unlike in the first movie, where he was a kind and genial old man, Toulon this time is depicted as a dangerous psychopath, an evil and malevolent zombie resurrected by the puppets, and whose sole aim is to kill the investigators of the Bodega Bay Inn. And this desire is only furthered by his crazy belief that one of the investigators is his wife incarnated.

Puppet Master 2 introduces a new puppet called Torch, a robotic doll that shoots flames out of his right hand. And the same haunting soundtrack from the first movie is reused here.

All in all, Puppet Master II is a fairly enjoyable, fun movie, although the plot is a little flat. Great ending too.

A third movie in the franchise was made, Puppet Master 3: Toulon's Revenge, in 1991. This time, the story takes a kind of retrospective angle, going back to Andre Toulon's roots, and is set in Berlin during WW II. The Nazi regime is trying to develop a drug that will animate dead people with a view to using them in the war effort. Andre Toulon is depicted in this movie as a Nazi dissident, who arouses the suspicions of the Germans. When Toulon's stunning wife is murdered, Toulon vows to exact his revenge on her killers. And who better to call on to fulfil that vengeance than his trusty, devilish little puppets?

Puppet Master 3 is one of the better instalments in the series, and is well worth a viewing. It also gives a highly entertaining, interesting insight into the events of WW II.

Puppet Master 4 (1994) brings the story right back into

modern times again. In this instalment, a young scientist, played by Gordon Currie, is working on an artificial science project in the Bodega Bay Inn when he is attacked by a gang of demons, who are out to kill him and thus end his research. By a strange (and very fortuitous) coincidence, one of the rooms the scientist uses just happens to house a mysterious case containing Toulon's notorious puppets. When the puppets are resurrected, they are used to battle the malevolent demons.

Puppet Master 4 introduces a new villain called THE TOTEM, in addition to a new puppet called Decapitron, whose appearance is modelled after Andre Toulon's outfit from Puppet Master 3: Toulon's Revenge. Little is known of Decapitron's background, but apparently he was an unfinished puppet that Toulon was working on while he was alive. Decapitron actually has the soul of Toulon inside him, which adds an interesting touch to the movie.

Puppet Master 5: The Final Chapter (now there's a misleading title if ever I heard one!), which was released in September 1994, stars Gordon Currie as the franchise's third Puppet Master and former Saint star Ian Ogilvy as his work colleague. The events take place just after Puppet Master 4. In the Bodega Bay Inn, the greedy Dr Jennings (Ogilvy) has arrived to steal Toulon's puppets in order to try and discover the secret of their animation. He hatches a plan which, he hopes, will make him rich quickly, and that is to sell the puppets' secrets as weapons of war. However, he has a lot of obstacles in his way to contend with, namely all the survivors from the previous movie: the puppets themselves, their saviour Gordon Currie, the Egyptian god Suketh, and Mr Totem.

Puppet Master 5, for me, is one of the weakest movies in

the series. There is scan gore here, it is not scary, and it just isn't as good as the previous movies. However, I suppose it's an OK movie to stick into your DVD player to while away a wet Sunday afternoon.

Puppet Master 6: Curse of the Puppet Master, released in 1998, is the first in the franchise to totally break continuity with all the previous movies, which is very annoying and disappointing. And as if that isn't enough, it's even worse than Puppet Master 5.

The storyline centres on a Dr Magrew (George Peck), the owner of a sideshow/museum, who now owns Toulon's puppets. Magrew and his daughter befriend a local simpleton called Tank. Noting his consummate skill in whittling, the pair persuade him to help them carve new puppets with a view to reanimating them. But the generic movie villain teenagers take a rather dim view of this, and embark on a spree of rape and aggression. As the movie progresses, we come to learn that this new Puppet Master's real aim is to kill Tank and use his life force to bring the puppet he was working on to life. By the time the daughter finds out his evil plan, it is too late, and once Tank becomes a puppet, all hell breaks loose.

The puppets don't really feature very much in this movie, instead playing second fiddle to a love triangle between a posh young woman, a rapist, and a (possibly) mentally handicapped person. It does not explain just how the story fits into the timeline of all the previous films. Even as a stand-alone movie, it makes no sense at all. It looks extremely cheap. The story is poor and disjointed. The performances are awful. There is no main protagonist, and no characters you can root for. The creature designs are laughable. And the movie's title belies the plot, for there is no actual curse, but just an old guy being a big jerk, and kidnapping mentally handicapped people with a view to murdering them. All in all, this movie is a big let down, and one that I certainly wouldn't add to my DVD collection. Avoid at all costs.

Retro Puppet Master (or Puppet Master 7) was released in 1999, and is a kind of throwback to the origins of Andre Toulon and the puppets very first adventure. During the days prior to his becoming the Puppet Master, the young Toulon (Greg Sestero) was running an avant-garde puppet theatre in pre-World War I Paris. At the same time, he was also involved in a romantic relationship with Ilsa, the beautiful daughter of the Swiss ambassador. When Toulon witnesses the cold-blooded murder of Afzel, an Egyptian sorcerer, who has stolen the "Secret of Life" from an ancient god, Sutekh, he is forced into a deadly struggle with the servants of Sutekh, who have kidnapped Ilsa. Consequently, Toulon and his puppets must ultimately confront the omnipotent power of an ancient god, in order to save the woman he loves. Will he succeed? Well, you'll have to watch the movie to find out.

Whilst Retro Puppet Master does explain how Toulon began practising the spell that breathes life into his puppets, it totally disregards what was originally established in the second film, which was exactly how he learned the power of animation. The film also saw Guy Rolfe's final appearance as Toulon, save for some flashback footage in The Legacy. The movie is more of a fantasy adventure than a straightforward horror movie and, as such, has become quite a controversial topic among fans of the series, many of them hating the storyline due to its lack of blood and gore and any real suspense.

Alan Toner

Puppet Master: The Legacy (2003) is the eighth movie in the franchise, and is regarded as the sequel to the 1994 film Puppet Master 5: The Final Chapter. It stars Jacob Witkin as an elderly Peter Hirtz (who appeared as a child character in Puppet Master 3: Toulon's Revenge) and Kate Orsini as an assassin, Maclain, hired to confront Hertz for information concerning the Puppet Master, Andre Toulon, and his animated puppets. This is certainly NOT a movie for anybody who hates flashbacks, because essentially that is just what the story mainly consists of. And these scenes are actually recycled ones from all the previous Puppet Master movies. The film also marks the final appearance of the original puppets constructed by David Allen and Dennis Gordon. Chronologically, apart from the more recent Puppet Master Axis films (of which more details later), this is the last movie in the series, although there has been talk of a possible revival of the franchise in the near future.

In the style of the old Universal monster-fest movies, there was actually a crossover film made involving Toulon's puppets, and that was Puppet Master vs Demonic Toys (2004). Well, I suppose it had to happen eventually, didn't it? Set on Christmas Eve, this movie stars Corey Feldman as Robert Toulon, the great grandnephew of Andre Toulon, who brings the puppets back to life with the help of his daughter, Alex (Danielle Keaton). Vanessa Angel also stars as Erica Sharpe, the corrupt boss of a toy-making factory, who has made an unholy deal with a demon called Bael. Sharpe's evil intention is to achieve world domination using the business's current line of holiday items: Christmas Pals, or demonic toys, set to cause complete havoc and bloodshed on Christmas Day. Consequently, a big puppets-vs-demonic toys confrontation ensues, as Toulon's group of now well-

Creepy Doll Movies

meaning puppets go head-to-head with Sharpe's band of devilish toys.

Puppet Master vs Demonic Toys was made for TV, and was first screened on the 18th December 2004. Many regard it as more of a holiday fun movie that all the family can watch, rather than an out-and-out horror flick. One good point in the movie's favour is that it doesn't resort to using a barrage of repeat scenes from previous Full Moon pictures, like some of the Puppet Master movies do. It is a totally new story, from beginning to end, which makes for a refreshing change. Granted, it's formulaic, it's cheesy, and it's a bit far fetched. But for all those failings, Puppet Master vs Demonic Toys is still a lot of fun to watch.

Puppet Master: Axis of Evil (2010) is another retrospective slant on the Puppet Master saga. Set during World War II, the story concerns a young man called Danny Coogan (Levi Fiehler), who, aided by Toulon's puppets (which he has discovered in a crate once owned by the old man), must tackle the Nazis who not only attacked his family and kidnapped his girlfriend, but are also planning to sabotage a secret American manufacturing plant. Can Danny and his band of powerful puppets put a stop to this Axis of Evil? Well, you'll have to watch the movie to find out.

The second, and final, Puppet Master Axis title to be released was Puppet Master: Axis Termination (2017). In this movie, we see our heroic but deadly band of puppets joining forces with a secret team of Allied Operatives, all of whom have psychic powers, to do battle with a new group of wicked Nazi enemies and their collection of malevolent Axis puppets. The outcome of this fight will be hugely critical, as it will decide the future of the free world.

Alan Toner

Coming right up to date with the Puppet Master franchise, a new movie has just been made, entitled Puppet Master: The Littlest Reich (2018). Written by S. Craig Zahler, the mastermind behind Bone Tomahawk and Brawl In Cell Block 99, and directed by Sonny Laguna and Tommy Wiklund, this latest instalment in the Puppet Master saga stars iconic scream queen Barbara Crampton as Carol Doreski, a police officer. The story basically concerns a recently divorced man called Edgar (Thomas Lennon), who returns to his childhood home only to find the puppet Blade in his dead brother's closet. Together with his friends, Ashley and Markowitz, Edgar sets out to a small-town convention in Oregon to sell the puppet for some quick cash during the 30th anniversary of the Toulon murders. Total chaos then breaks out during the auction when a mysterious, malevolent force, as old as time itself, brings to life all of the puppets throughout the convention and makes them go on a bloody killing spree. Even the man who started it all, the irrepressible Andre Toulon, pops up again in this film, this time as an evil monster.

Puppet Master: The Littlest Reich is considered to be something of a reboot of the original Puppet Master movie. It's also the first film in the series that does not include the Jester puppet. But whether it will enjoy the same degree of cult success and fan-love as the first movie did remains to be seen.

In October 2017, fans of the Puppet Master franchise got a real treat, for a huge, stunning metal-and-wood replica of Andre Toulon's travelling case, containing all 11 Puppet Master movies, was released by Full Moon Pictures under the title "The Ultimate Puppet Master Collectable Trunk". In addition to all the movies, the trunk also contained a mini

Creepy Doll Movies

Blade figure, a collectible booklet, glorious new cover artwork for each film, and much more.

5. Robert The Doll

The best British haunted doll movie of recent times, at least for me, has to be Robert. Made in 2015 and directed by Andrew Jones, the film is based on real life events, and tells the story of an ordinary family's supernatural experiences after their son is given a vintage doll called Robert by their former, much disgruntled housekeeper.

Paul (Lee Bane) and Jenny (Suzie Frances Garton) lead a very active life, and so they employ a housekeeper, Agatha (Judith Haley) to take the domestic load off them a bit. Unfortunately, now being of advancing years, the housekeeper has trouble remembering things. Consequently, after discussing the matter carefully, Paul and Jenny decide it would be better to let her go. Naturally, Agatha is not too pleased about this, but asks the couple if they would allow her to give their son Gene (Flynn Allen) a last goodbye, to which they agree. Before she departs, she gives him an old doll named Robert. After she leaves, mysterious things start to happen all around the house, and Gene keeps attributing these incidents to his doll, Robert.

Jenny starts to believe that something is definitely wrong with the doll, but Paul is not convinced and thinks she's just imagining it all, due to the medical condition she has been suffering with. Her mental problems have also put a big strain on their relationship. As things began to deteriorate in the household, and as these strange happenings start to turn dangerous, the family eventually have to stop their bickering, be strong, and band together in order to face and, hopefully, eradicate the untold evil that seems to have completely taken over their home.

One of the things I especially loved about Robert was the general appearance of the doll itself. Designed by Sharron Jones and Susan Mitchell, they created a character that really perturbs you each time you look at it, those huge eyes seeming to bore down into your very soul. Granted, the doll does very little in the film except sit around, but the way the characters interact with each other, coupled with a storyline that builds and builds the suspense to a quite creepy level, makes for a very entertaining and memorable movie indeed. I know a lot of critics have panned this film, describing it as "corny" and "slow", but of course I don't agree, as I think Robert is one of the more enjoyable creepy doll movies ever made. And being a big fan of British horror movies, I am always pleased to see new homegrown fright flicks produced which don't, unlike a lot of the American horror movies, just rely on sex-mad, foul-mouthed, formulaic teens in order to gain cheap scares. So yes, I would definitely give Robert a 10 out of 10.

Despite similarities to the popular Child's Play franchise, the movie Robert is in fact based on a real-life, supposedly cursed doll named Robert. The doll belonged to a painter and author named Robert Eugene Otto, and is now exhibited in the East Martello Museum, in Key West, Florida. Both the actual doll and the movie doll are dressed in a sailor uniform. Nevertheless, the movie is purely a work of fiction, with a story loosely based on the real life doll.

As I enjoyed Robert so much, you can imagine my joy when I discovered that they had made a sequel. The Curse of Robert was released in 2016, and proved to be equally as enjoyable as the first movie. This one follows on directly from its predecessor, introducing a cash-strapped student, Emily Barker (Tiffany Ceri), who takes on a night shift job at a local museum. However, her nocturnal duty is soon rudely interrupted when she starts hearing strange footsteps walking down empty corridors and witnesses acts of what appear to be wanton vandalism in various parts of the building. She attributes these disturbances to a rather creepy-looking vintage doll called Robert, whom she believes has somehow taken on a life of its own and is creeping around the building, wreaking havoc in the small hours. When she reports her experiences to both the head of security and the museum owner, neither of them believes her. But when members of the night staff start turning up dead under strange circumstances, Emily becomes certain that this is definitely the work of the doll.

A local police detective (Steven Dolton) begins to suspect that Emily is behind the murders, and she is shocked to find herself the prime suspect in the investigation. So begins a stressful, tortuous effort for Emily to try and clear her name, and to attempt to convince people that it really is the doll that is responsible for the string of brutal murders, and not her. But will even Emily herself eventually fall victim to the Curse of Robert the Doll?

The Curse of Robert is a really well done, fun movie, and is every bit as gripping and entertaining as the first one, unlike so many horror movie sequels these days. I liked the way they moved the location of Robert's creepy exploits from a domestic to a museum environment. It was also good to see a return of the mother (Suzie Frances Garton) from the first Robert film, although it's a rather sad and brief appearance, as she is now confined to a mental asylum, having been traumatised by the events of the first movie.

Unfortunately, I can't utter the same superlatives for the third Robert movie, The Toymaker (2017), as I can for the first two. This one was definitely the worst of the three, and I hated it so much that I decided not to add it to my other Robert movies to complete the trilogy, which is a shame, as I'd been expecting this third instalment to be just as good as the others. This time, in the style of the Puppetmaster movies (actually, this movie IS a bit too similar to the Puppetmaster films for my liking), the story takes a retrospective spin on the Robert saga, transporting us back to 1941 Nazi Germany. Hitler's henchmen are in pursuit of the titular Toymaker, who has a mystical book that gives life to inanimate objects. As the Nazis terrorize the locals while they search high and low for the book, the Toymaker experiments with the ancient tome and succeeds in giving life to his collection of vintage dolls. When one of his employees betrays him, the Toymaker's shop is raided by the Nazis, who steal the book and kidnap Amos. But the animated dolls and toys are livid at the loss of their master. A mission is then launched to rescue the Toymaker from the clutches of the nefarious Colonel Ludolf Von Alvensleben, and exact a brutal and bloody revenge on the Nazis.

On the whole, The Toymaker is an extremely slow, dull affair, with a very poor, sometimes laughable, storyline. There is far too much chat in it (I am afraid that six people speaking inside a room for 30 minutes is guaranteed to soon send me to sleep), and in fact you don't see either the Toymaker or Robert the Doll for nearly half an hour. It should never have been made, as it completely detracts from the hitherto entertaining aspect of the Robert franchise.

At the time of writing this book, I see that they have just made a fourth movie in the Robert series, entitled The Revenge of Robert (2018). From what I have read of the descriptions, this movie is again set in Nazi Germany, only this time most of the action apparently takes place onboard a train. To judge by these blurbs, this new film doesn't seem so divorced from its predecessor, so if the storyline is as bad as the other one, then I think I'll pass!

The actual Robert the Doll, which is said to be haunted, is now located at the East Martello Museum in Key West, Florida, USA. The doll is annually rotated to the Old Post Office and Customhouse in Key West during the month of October. The doll used in the movie is NOT the doll on display in Key West.

6. Magic

Magic (1978), which starred Anthony Hopkins as a rather schizophrenic ventriloquist, is one of my all time favourite creepy doll movies. So reminiscent of the ventriloquist doll segment in Dead of Night, and based on a novel by William Goldman, Magic has a high rewatchabiliy factor, the performances of not only Anthony Hopkins, but also those of Burgess Meredith and Ann Margaret enhancing the brilliant, highly entertaining and gripping storyline.

Directed by Richard Attenborough and based on Goldman's screenplay, Magic tells the story of Charles "Corky" Withers (Anthony Hopkins), who is a complete disaster when performing his first real attempt at being a professional magician. His mentor "Merlin" (E. J. André) says that he needs to have a better show business gimmick.

A year later, Corky returns as a combination magician and ventriloquist, with a rather abrasive and foul-mouthed dummy called Fats. The act soon starts going down really well with audiences. Corky's influential agent, Ben Greene (Burgess Meredith), is just about to sign him up for his own television show, but Corky runs away with Fats to his hometown of Catskills, on the pretext that he fears success. But in reality, Corky is very unwilling to take the TV network's required medical examination for fear of doctors finding out that he suffers from severe mental problems, and that even off-stage he cannot control Fats (who seems to be an eerie manifestation of Corky's personality). In Catskills, Corky meets an old love from high school days, Peggy (Ann-Margret).

Corky persuades Peggy to leave her dysfunctional marriage, but Fats, who seems to be now taking on a mind of his own, totally disapproves of the relationship. As the tension increases, Corky must learn to control Fats and regain his own sanity before it's too late.

Alongside the role of Hannibal Lecter, I would regard Anthony Hopkins's performance as Corky, the schizo ventriloquist, as one of his best ever. Of course, given his iconic status in the world of cinema, comparisons are always going to be drawn between Lecter and Corky, for both characters constantly totter on the edge of complete madness. But whilst Lecter can control it fairly well, Corky is always a helpless, malleable pawn under the influence of his malevolent, controlling alter ego, and I think it is this trait of vulnerability that adds a certain outstanding quality to the film.

Magic is a quintessential psychological thriller of the highest degree, and one that every lover of creepy ventriloquist movies should have in their movie collection. It is also a film that has so much to offer to the viewer at different levels, with its multi-layered storyline. Far more sophisticated than straightforward creepy doll movies like Child's Play. Granted, the melodrama does tend to outweigh the horror element, but most scenes involving Hopkins and Fats the dummy are certainly powerful enough to resonate with you for years. The late, great Sir Richard Attenborough must be utterly congratulated for giving us a movie that has proved to be such a timeless classic, and such a firm favourite with thousands of genre fans throughout the world.

7. Anna

Based on a screenplay by Gerald Crum, Anna (2017) tells the story of two brothers, Jacob (Justin Duncan) and Shawn (Gerald Crum), who host a YouTube channel on the subject of the paranormal. One of their investigations sees them visiting reportedly haunted locations or interacting with various objects said to be cursed. Whilst the footage has never really produced any real solid evidence for the existence of the supernatural, the pair continues to promise viewers that their experiences are genuine. And they have something really "special" for their next video: they've borrowed (or, to be more precise, nicked) a doll from a paranormal museum called Anna, a doll which is said to carry a curse about it and which, they hope, will boost their viewing figures.

    The brothers take the doll to a reputedly haunted house, hoping to get as much paranormal activity going as possible, using Anna as a catalyst for seven days. However, the movie makes you start wondering if all the stories of the haunted house are just nonsense, or if they really are true.

    The problem with this film is that the comedic elements tend to dilute the horror ones to a most annoying extent. Also, Anna does not really give much of an impression as a proper, cursed, scary doll. She's just an ugly, mucky, used doll, and it's so laughable to see the first victim showering her with love, despite her unpalatable appearance.

Alan Toner

All in all, Anna is a rather boring, dull and unmemorable film, and one that has attracted a lot of criticism by genre fans. The acting is awful and the dialogue equally so. Even the high body count and spot of nudity doesn't save it from slumping to a level of utter mediocrity.

Avoid Anna like the plague, as it really is one of the worst creepy doll movies ever made.

8. Asylum – Mannikins of Horror

Asylum is a 1972 British horror anthology movie, produced by Amicus. Based on a script by Robert Bloch and directed by Roy Ward Baker, Asylum features four tales of horror, each of which concerns an inmate of the titular asylum, and a framing story featuring Robert Powell as Dr Martin, who arrives at the asylum for a job interview with the wheelchair-bound, authoritarian Dr Rutherford (Patrick Magee). But as this book is wholly about creepy dolls, it is just the fourth (and last) story that will be covered here, and that is "Mannikins of Horror", which features Herbert Lom as the highly intellectual, but obviously twisted, Dr Byron and his odd range of self-made "mannikins".

When Martin interviews Dr. Byron, he finds that the inmate holds Rutherford in deep contempt. Byron explains he is working on a project involving soul transference with a small automaton, whose head is a stunning likeness of his own. He then shows Martin several earlier examples of his work. Byron plans to "will" his mannikins to life simply by the power of his mind. He explains that the interior of the robot is organic, a miniaturised version of his own insides. When Martin concludes his interview with the deranged doctor, Max, the attendant, takes him back downstairs to give his opinion on the inmates to Rutherford.

In the meantime, lying there in his cell and staring intently at a doll that has his own face, Byron succeeds in bringing his mannikin to life. The mentally controlled doll then shuffles robotically towards Rutherford's office, creeps up behind him whilst he is talking to Martin, and stabs him in the back of a neck with a scalpel, killing him instantly. Shocked and horrified, Martin jumps up and immediately destroys the mannequin, stamping on it to reveal its glistening-red innards, which results in the death of Dr. Byron.

Herbert Lom is just brilliant in this segment as the sinister Dr Byron, whose outward appearance of politeness and hospitality is belied by his dark, malevolent inner streak. The way he manipulates his "Mannikins of Horror", simply by using the power of thought, is just so entertaining and original. And although this, the last story in the movie, does not really have a flashback story (unlike the others), it complements the movie superbly, has an intriguing premise, and leads up to a great finale.

9. The Creepy Doll

The Creepy Doll was a 2011 budget horror movie. The story introduces to a newlywed couple, Jason and Kate Carroway, who have just moved back to Jason's hometown. Kate comes from a broken home, and has a huge collection of antique dolls, with which she is utterly obsessed.

There is one doll in particular in Kate's collection that seems to be the most significant: a rather sinister-looking doll, with one ruined eye that is permanently open, and a cute mouth that looks as if it wants to swallow you whole. And Kate is also deeply resentful of Jason's childhood friend, Emily, who is always showing up in their lives. Her feelings of jealousy may indeed be justified, for Jason and Emily were once engaged, a fact starkly revealed by the wall in Jason's Mom's house that is just filled with pictures of the former lovers.

It's not long before Jason notices his bride slowly turning into someone he doesn't recognize. Is it the doll that is behind his wife's sudden bizarre change in personality, or is she just going crazy? Well, I am not giving anything away here, so you'll to watch the movie to find out.

The main strength of The Creepy Doll is that it takes the traditional monster of the creepy mannikin trope and effectively interweaves its supernatural tale of an evil doll with a domestic drama of a jealous (and possibly batty) wife, so that The Creepy Doll delivers on both dramatic levels,

Alan Toner

each supporting and playing off the other.

10. Dead Silence

Dead Silence (2007) is James Wan's follow up to Saw (2004), and is one of the spookiest creepy doll movies I have ever seen.

Dead Silence follows the story of Jamie Ashen (Ryan Kwanten), who, after receiving a mysterious puppet, returns home to find his wife, Lisa (Laura Regan) murdered. With a detective (Donnie Wahlberg) convinced he is the murderer, Jamie returns to his childhood town of Raven's Fair, where a legendary ghost story is told. The story is about a woman named Mary Shaw, a ventriloquist who went mad in the 1940s after being suspected of kidnapping a young boy who heckled one of her performances by labelling her a fraud. Accused of murdering the boy, Shaw was hunted down by the townspeople, who exacted a brutal and bloody revenge by cutting out Shaw's tongue before killing her. Shaw was then buried with her huge collection of vaudeville dolls and puppets, and the townspeople believed that they had now silenced her forever. But, as it turned out, how wrong they were!

After her death, it seems that Shaw has been taking revenge on the townspeople from beyond the grave, when numerous families are found dead with their tongues missing. Jamie takes it upon himself to solve the legend and curse before he becomes the next victim.

Although some critics have dismissed Dead Silence as

nothing more than just another formulaic, clichéd horror movie about a loopy ventriloquist, the film is nevertheless highly regarded by many horror fans, and there are certainly enough horror tropes to keep them satisfied here: cackling, creepy old ladies; singing children; flickering lights; photos of deceased family members; copious thunder and lightning; open coffins; beckoning spirits; and, of course, creepy dolls. And to top all of this, the movie has an overpowering, appreciable sense of evil and menace throughout. It is also a superb throwback to the golden age of fright films, like the kind of movies that were made by William Castle and that starred Vincent Price. It also has a brilliant twist at the end.

In short, although Dead Silence is a movie that is really enjoyable and fun, it is definitely NOT the sort that I would advise you to watch all on your own, late at night, if you are the kind of person who is easily frightened – especially by creepy old ladies and weird dolls.

11. Dolly Dearest

Dolly Dearest is an American black comedy made in 1991, set in the gorgeous background of Mexico. Starring Rip Torn and Denise Crosby, it tells the tale of an American family, the Wades, who, with their two children, take up residence in the area and reopen a factory - The Dolly Dearest Manufacturing Company - of dolls in a site based close to an archaeological area, which has a dark history.

Years ago, in Mexico, an archaeologist released the evil spirit of a demonic child from a tomb of an ancient Mayan tribe called Sanzia, said to be worshippers of the Devil. When Sanzia dies in an accident, its spirit is released upon the earth, and it possesses not only the couple's little girl, Jessie (Candy Hutson), but also a number of the dolls in the factory.

Dolly Dearest could be regarded as the Mexican feminisation of "Child's Play", as there are quite a few similarities here to the Chucky movie.

Dolly Dearest was one of those mediocre films that did boast some good effects, but nevertheless still wasn't really all that frightening, except to maybe a very young child. It takes a full half hour to really get going. The acting was okay, but the characters were very irritating, and rather stereotyped. And it was laughable how the mother (Denise Crosby) allowed her daughter to do whatever she liked, and didn't even suspect that the girl was, cunningly and devilishly, manipulating her. Furthermore, although the doll itself was creepy to a degree, the movie's script was extremely derivative of similar creepy doll/child flicks.

These failings class Dolly Dearest in my lower rank of creepy doll movies, I'm afraid, and that is why I have passed on adding this lame effort to my collection.

12. Dolls

Dolls (1987) has always been a big favourite among fans of creepy doll movies. Written by Ed Naha, produced by Charles Band and Brian Yuzna, and directed by Stuart Gordon, Dolls centres on two wealthy snobs who go on a vacation with their daughter. Their journey is interrupted when a violent storm hits and their car becomes stuck in the mud. As a result, they decide to seek refuge for the night in a nearby old mansion (shades of the Karloff 1932 classic The Old Dark House here).

Moments later, three other people wander into the house: Ralph, a man who doesn't seem to have grown up much, and two punk rock girls whom he gave a lift to. Little do they all know that this is a mansion that harbours a dark secret: dolls that come to life. And dolls that murder people, indiscriminately and viciously.

Dolls is a movie replete with all the typical horror tropes: a dark and stormy night; a creepy, sprawling old mansion, with dark hallways filled with antiques; a pair of batty, weird old timers who are the owners of the mansion and who also happen to be doll makers.

The film eventually reveals that the puppetmaker's puppets in the house are actually cursed immoral people who had been killed and imprisoned in puppet bodies for years in order to pay for their crimes.

All in all, Dolls is a very atmospheric movie that is great

Alan Toner

fun to watch, and certainly one that deserves to be added to your creepy doll collection.

13. Trilogy of Terror

Now we come to a movie that is definitely one of my all time favourite anthology flicks in terms of offering a real, good, fun creepy doll story. That movie is Trilogy of Terror (1975), starring the lovely Karen Black, who features in all three of the segments here.

Originally made for American TV only and directed by Dan Curtis, Trilogy of Terror was first aired as an ABC Movie of the Week on 4th March 1975. It has one of the most terrifying and truly unforgettable creepy dolls that have ever graced creepy doll movie history: a Zuni fetish doll, crafted in the form of a misshapen aboriginal warrior equipped with razor sharp teeth and a spear. This lethal little doll features in the last story of the trilogy, which is called "Amelia", and is based on a short story by Richard Matheson titled "Prey". Once again, Karen Black is the main protagonist here, playing the titular character who lives all alone in a high-rise apartment building.

Returning home after a shopping spree, Amelia is carrying a package containing the said Zuni fetish doll. A scroll comes with the doll, claiming that the doll contains the actual spirit of a Zuni hunter named "He Who Kills", and that the gold chain adorning the doll confines the spirit.

As Amelia makes a call to her mother, it becomes clear that she shares her mother's overbearing behaviour. Amelia struggles to justify her independence and cancels their plans for the evening by claiming she has a date. As Amelia leaves the room, we see that the Zuni doll's golden chain has somehow fallen off.

Some time later, Amelia is preparing a meal, using a carving knife. She enters the darkened living room, noting that the doll is not on the coffee table. Then she hears a noise in the kitchen, and when she investigates, the knife has gone missing. Returning to the living room, she is suddenly attacked by the doll, which stabs at her ankles viciously. Despite her attempts to escape, the doll chases her all around the apartment.

In the bathroom, Amelia envelops the doll in a towel and attempts, unsuccessfully, to drown it in the bathtub. She later traps it in a suitcase, but the doll manages to free itself by cutting a circular hole through the top of suitcase with the butcher knife.

After several more vicious attacks, Amelia manages to hurl the doll into the oven. Capturing her breath, she stands there listening to its howls and screams of agony as it burns. Soon the screams abate and eventually stop. Amelia then opens the oven to ensure that the doll is "dead", and a cloud of black smoke billows out. As she inhales the smoke, she is suddenly overcome.

Some later on, we see Amelia, from behind, place another call to her mother in a calm, steady voice. She apologises for her behaviour during the previous call, and invites her mother around to her place for dinner. She then tears the bolt from her front door and crouches low to the ground in a kind of feral manner, hiding in the corner and clutching a carving knife. As the view of her moves to a frontal one, we see her continually stabbing at the floor with the weapon, grinning manically and showing the terrifying teeth of the Zulu warrior, whose spirit seems to have now taken over Amelia's body.

What a brilliant ending to a brilliant story! I always love to revisit Trilogy of Terror, if only to once again be entertained by this gripping tale of an evil Zulu warrior doll on the rampage through the apartment of a helpless woman all alone. And I am so excited by the fact that Trilogy of Terror is soon going to be released on glorious Blu Ray by Kino Lorber. Needless to say, I shall definitely be adding that to my collection!

A sequel to the movie, Trilogy of Terror II, was made in 1996, although this film is very hard to get on DVD. The third story in the trilogy, "He Who Kills" sees the return of the bloodthirsty Zuni fetish doll, this time menacing a female doctor (Lysette Anthony), who is assigned by the police to examine the doll following the double homicide of Amelia and her mother from the first movie. Needless to say, the doll comes back to life, and once again all hell breaks loose.

I do very much hope they eventually release Trilogy of Terror II on Blu Ray at some point in the future, as it would be great to have these two classic anthology movies in my collection.

14. Annabelle

Annabelle the doll made her very first appearance in the James Wan 2013 horror movie The Conjuring. Since the release of that film, Annabelle has gone on to appear in several more movies in The Conjuring universe and, as a result, has gained something of a cult status with genre fans.

The Annabelle doll is based on the real life case of a Raggedy Ann doll, which was nowhere near as scary in appearance as the porcelain one in the movie. The real Annabelle was given to Donna, a student nurse, by her mother as a birthday gift in 1970. The mother had bought the doll from a hobby store. Donna was living with her friend Angie at the time, and was naturally delighted with her gift. But that delight didn't last for long, for strange things started happening in the girls' home, things that led the two friends to suspect that the doll might be behind them.

The doll would start to move around on its own, only occasional movements at first, but then movements that increased in frequency. And then the weirdness accelerated, for the girls started to find notes scattered around their apartment. Even weirder, the notes had been written on parchment paper, which neither of the girls had ever used. The notes said various things, but the most common messages written were "Help Lou" and "Help Us". Apparently, and chillingly, the doll could not only move, but could actually write as well.

Creepy Doll Movies

At their wit's end, the girls finally contacted a medium and a séance was held in the apartment. The spirit of an Annabelle Higgins came through, whose story the medium related to the girls. Annabelle was a young girl who had once lived on the property before the apartments were built. Her dead body was found in the field on which the apartment complex was constructed. She was just seven years old.

The spirit told the medium that she felt relaxed and at peace with Donna and Angie, and wanted to stay with them. Feeling sympathy for Annabelle, Donna gave her permission to inhabit the doll and stay with them. They were to soon find out, however, that Annabelle was not what she appeared to be, and was definitely no ordinary doll.

The girls' long-time friend, Lou, had a very bad experience with the doll, including mysterious claw marks inflicted on his chest, which drew blood. This was the final straw for occupants of the apartment, and Donna had no alternative but to summon somebody who was of higher authority in regard to getting rid of demonic spirits. The priests she contacted referred her to Ed and Lorraine Warren, the famous ghost hunting team who have investigated numerous hauntings over the years, including The Amityville Horror case.

When the Warrens investigated the case, they concluded that the doll itself was not possessed, but manipulated by an inhuman presence. It seemed that this particular spirit was using the doll to create the illusion that it was alive. At the end of the investigation, the Warrens requested that a priest, Father Cooke, perform an exorcism rite in the apartment to cleanse it of all evil forces. Once the exorcism was over, Donna requested that the Warrens take the big Raggedy Ann doll with them, just in case the supernatural force reared its ugly head again. The doll is now a permanent exhibit, kept in a glass case, in the Warren Occult Museum.

In regard to the Annabelle doll featured in the movie The Conjuring, well, just like in the real life case aforementioned, this doll wreaks similar havoc on those all around her. The movie centres on the true-life Perron family, who claimed that they experienced both friendly and malevolent spirits in their Rhode Island farmhouse in 1971. Patrick Wilson and Vera Farmiga star as Ed and Lorraine Warren, paranormal investigators and authors famously associated with sensational cases of hauntings. The Warrens visit the Perron family, in the hope that they can help them to eradicate whatever entities are haunting their farmhouse. What the Warrens discover is a whole area steeped in a satanic haunting that is now targeting the Perron family wherever they go. To banish this evil, the Warrens will have to summon all their skills and spiritual strength to defeat this spectral menace at its source before it destroys everyone involved.

The Conjuring is a movie full of extremely creepy and disturbing scenes. The part that freaked me out the most was where Carolyn Perron gets possessed by the spirit of Bathsheba (the accused witch to whom the farmhouse once belonged, and who sacrificed her week-old child to the devil and killed herself in 1863 after cursing all who would take her land), complete with bag over head and blood spurts beneath the material that would give anybody nightmares for months. What jump scares there are in the movie are cleverly spaced out, so that they don't detract too much from the general atmosphere of unease and tension that pervades the story. Granted, The Conjuring is a film that is certainly not without its fair share of haunted house clichés - strange odours, creepy and dark cellars, creaking doors and so on – but for all that, the movie delivers brilliantly in the scare factor stakes, thanks to Wan's excellent directing. And Joseph Bishara's musical score complements the movie brilliantly.

The Conjuring was released in the United States and Canada on July 19, 2013, and received positive reviews from critics. It grossed over $319 million worldwide against its $20 million budget. A sequel, The Conjuring 2, was released on June 10, 2016, with a third film currently in development.

In regard to Annabelle (2014), this movie is a kind of prequel to The Conjuring. The setting of this film is in the 1960s in a California suburb, and centres on a young couple, John and Mia Form, who are expecting their first child. John (Ward Horton) has found the ideal present for his doll-collecting wife, Mia (Annabelle Wallis): a lovely, rare vintage doll clad in a pure white wedding dress, with a painted ivory face. However, Mia's delight with Annabelle is short lived, for one terrifying night, members of a satanic cult break into their home and brutally attack the couple. But bloodshed and terror are not the only things the cultists leave behind, for they have evoked an entity so evil and demonic that nothing they did will equal the horrifying malevolence that the doll Annabelle is about to unleash on the couple, especially after she gives birth to their daughter, Leah.

In The Conjuring, Annabelle took more of a minor role, appearing only at the pre-opening credits sequence, whereas in Annabelle she features more prominently, and we get to know much more about her and how she first came to be demonically possessed.

Although Annabelle is a bit of a slow burn, the tension and horror do eventually kick in later on in the film, with the ever-so-creepy-looking Annabelle doll exerting its evil influence on the couple to a most disturbing extent. I suppose you could describe it as a movie with a mixture of Helter Skelter, Amityville Horror and Chucky elements thrown in. And the film certainly doesn't need CGI (none of which seem to be evident at all in this film) to pull off all the necessary thrills and chills, for instead it relies on simple old school horror with all the relevant tropes: darkened apartment, furniture being moved around by unseen hands, figure standing in the shadows, and so on. For me, these tropes are far scarier than some formulaic special effects we have seen a hundred times over.

Another good thing I liked about the movie was the excellent cinematography that employs camera angles that give you the point of view of the tormented victim, so that you are unsure about what will happen next. Although Annabelle is not a horror movie that one would rate as a groundbreaking classic, like Rosemary's Baby or The Exorcist, it is still a lot of fun to watch, and a good addition to The Conjuring universe.

When I heard that they were making a sequel to Annabelle, I was, as you can imagine, really thrilled, especially after having enjoyed the previous movie so much. However, when I did eventually view Annabelle: Creation (2017), I was very disappointed. The movie was nowhere near as entertaining as the first Annabelle film, and there were times during this car crash of a sequel that I just felt like reaching for the OFF switch. I mean, honestly, it was that bad. The story, for what it's worth, centres on a nun and several girls from a shuttered orphanage, who are welcomed into the home of a doll maker and his wife, whose daughter tragically died twelve years ago. It's not long before the nun

Creepy Doll Movies

and the girls become prime targets of the doll maker's hellish creation: Annabelle.

Apparently a prequel to Annabelle, the plot makes absolutely no sense whatsoever. And as if that isn't bad enough, all the characters, despite being children, never really act like a normal person would act in a similar situation, making stupid decision after stupid decision. The movie was also disappointingly devoid of real scares and gore. It was also annoyingly littered with horror clichés. Watching paint dry would have been more exciting, to be quite blunt.

I don't want to go on any more about this utterly tedious and boring mess of a movie. Suffice to say that it is one you should avoid like the plague, as it really is a huge let down after the much more entertaining Annabelle.

15. Twilight Zone's Talky Tina

Whilst I do realise that, unlike all the others in the book, this final chapter does not cover a complete creepy doll movie as such, but instead just a short segment of a TV show, I nevertheless deem this story to be so good, memorable and chilling that I felt I just had to round off this book with a tale that, for me, utterly sums up just how downright CREEPY some dolls can be, be they in films or in TV programmes.

The doll to which I refer is called "Living Doll", and was featured in Episode 6 of Season 5 of The Twilight Zone. First screened in 1963, "Living Doll" features Telly Savalas (of Kojak fame, alongside all his other movie credits), who plays Erich Streator, a rather overbearing and icy stepfather to his wife Annabelle (now where have we heard THAT name before?) and stepdaughter Christie. When Annabelle buys Christie a new Talky Tina doll, Erich soon displays his utter disapproval and irritation. I mean, this guy just doesn't seem to want his family to enjoy anything that a normal family should. The cruel stepfather is really personified by Savalas here.

"My name is Talky Tina, and I love you very much," coos Tina cutely whenever her string is pulled. But whenever she's alone with Erich, that cuteness soon evaporates as she says other, more ominous phrases, starting with "I don't think I like you" and quickly escalating to "I'm

Creepy Doll Movies

going to kill you."

Erich starts to suspect that his wife could be behind it all, an accusation she vehemently denies. Frustrated, he tries to get rid of the doll by any means open to him, but it always seems to defiantly reappear - and also seems intent on carrying out its threats. Thus a constant battle of wits ensues between the grumpy step dad and the apparently supernaturally manipulated doll. Who is going to win in the end? Well, I won't spoil the ending by revealing it, as you will have to watch the episode yourself to find out.

Although some genre fans might compare "Living Doll" to modern-day creepy doll movies like the Child's Play franchise, it has a great concept which, coupled with Telly Savalas's brilliant performance as the hateful stepfather, still makes for a highly entertaining and gripping half-hour. The Twilight Zone turned out some great little stories in its time, and I would certainly rate "Living Doll" as one of the best episodes ever.

Author's Note

If you enjoyed this book, I would really appreciate it if you could leave a review for it on Amazon.

You can also subscribe to my Newsletter at: https://bit.ly/2rDvlLB

Twitter Profile: Scouselad8
Facebook Profile: mersey.male1

Alan Toner
www.alantoner.com

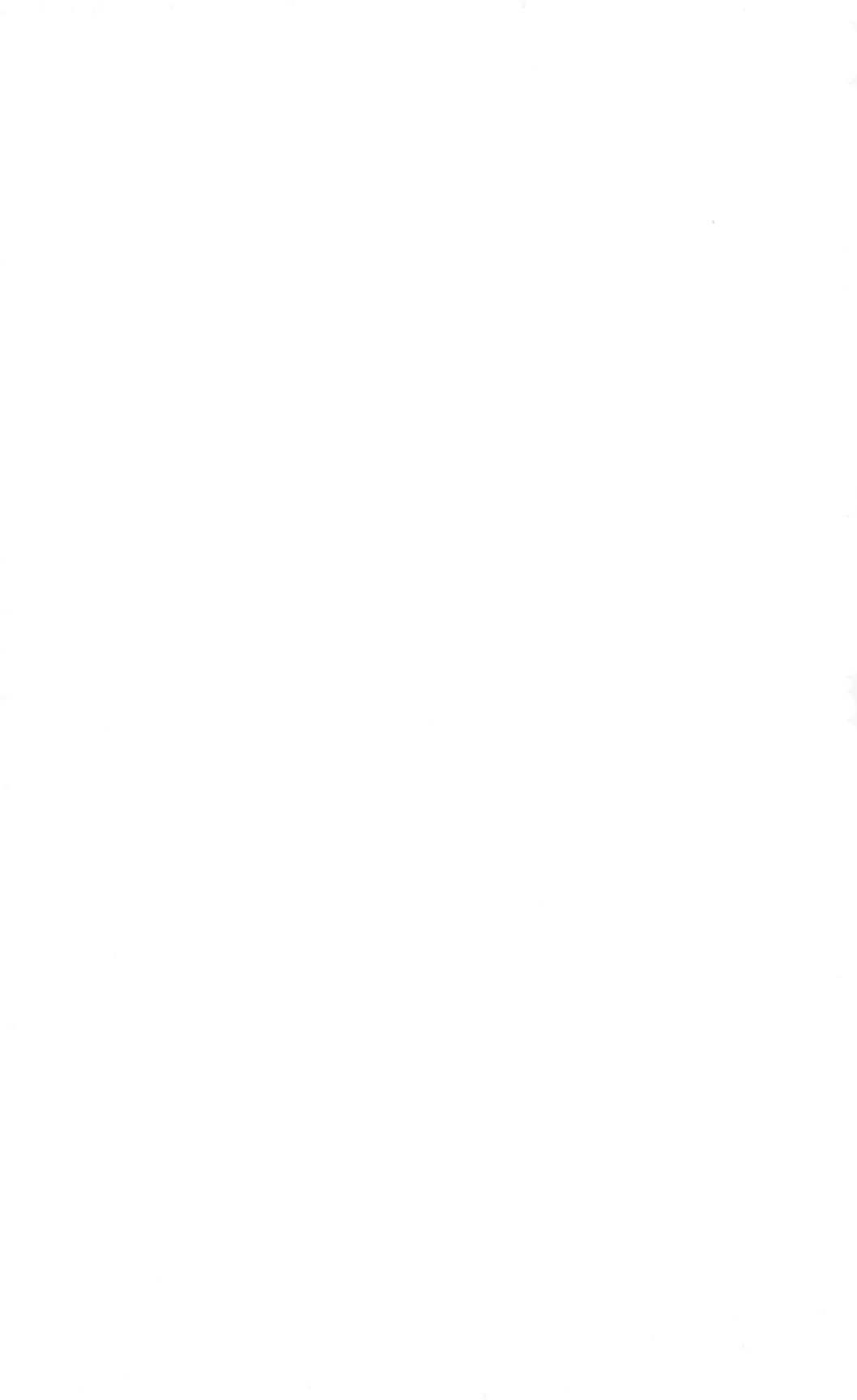

www.ingramcontent.com/pod-product-compliance
Lightning Source LLC
Chambersburg PA
CBHW071432220526
45469CB00004B/1499